Robert McCloskey's

HOMER PRICE

Teacher Guide

MEMORIA PRESS

www.MemoriaPress.com

Robert McCloskey's
HOMER PRICE

TEACHER GUIDE

Contributing Authors: Leigh Lowe, Brenda Janke, Brittany Mann, & Anne Parry

ISBN 978-1-61538-081-7

Cover Illustration: Starr Steinbach

Contents

PREPARING TO READ:

REVIEW

- Orally review any previous vocabulary.
- Review the plot of the book as read so far.
- Periodically review the concepts of character, setting, and plot.

STUDY GUIDE PREVIEW

- Reading Notes:
    - Read aloud together.
    - This section gives the student key characters, places, and terms that are relevant to a particular time period, etc.
- Vocabulary:
    - Read aloud together so that students will recognize words when they come across them in their reading.
    - Look at each word within the context that it is used, and help your student come up with the best synonym that defines the word. (Make sure it is a synonym the student knows the meaning of.)
    - Record the word's meaning in the students' study guides. (Use students' knowledge of Latin and other vocabulary to decipher meanings.)
- Comprehension Questions:
    - Read through these questions with students to encourage purposeful reading.

READING:

- Student reads the chapter (or selection of the chapter for that lesson) independently or to the teacher (for younger students).
- For younger students, you can alternate between teacher-read and student-read passages. Model good reading skills. Encourage students to read expressively and smoothly. The teacher may occasionally take oral reading grades.
- While reading, mark each vocabulary word as you come across it.
- Have students take note in their study guide margin of pages where a Comprehension Question is answered.

AFTER READING:

COMPREHENSION QUESTIONS

- Older students can answer these questions independently, but younger students (2nd-4th) need to answer the questions orally, form a good sentence, and then write it down, using correct punctuation, capitalization, and spelling. (You may want to write the sentence down for the younger student after forming it orally, and then let the student copy it perfectly.)
- It is not necessary to write the answer to every question; some may be better answered orally. Just make sure you answer the questions that will appear on tests so that students will have the information they need to study.
- Answering questions and composing answers is a valuable learning activity. Questions require students to think; writing a concise answer is a good composition exercise.

QUOTATIONS AND DISCUSSION QUESTIONS

- Use the Quotations and Discussion Questions section of each lesson as a guide to your oral discussion of the key concepts in the chapter that may not be covered in the comprehension questions.
- These talking points can take your oral discussion to a higher level than covered in the students' written work. Use this time as an opportunity to introduce higher-level thinking. You can introduce concepts the students may not be mature enough to fully understand yet but that would be beneficial for them to begin thinking about.
- A key to the Discussion Questions is in the back of the Teacher Guide.

ENRICHMENT

- The Enrichment activities include composition, copywork, dictation, research, mapping, drawing, poetry work, literary terms, and more.
- This section has a variety of activities in it, but the most valuable activity is composition. Your student should complete at least one composition assignment each week. Proof student's work and have student copy composition until grammatically perfect. Insist on clear, concise writing. For younger students, start with 2-3 sentences, and do the assignment together. The student can form good sentences orally as you write them down, and then the student copies them.
- These activities can be completed as time and interest allow. Do not feel you need to complete all of these activities. Choose the ones that you feel are the best use of your students' time.

UNIT REVIEW AND TESTS

- There is a unit review and a quiz or test following every few lessons (varies by individual guide).
- On the weeks that have these reviews and tests, you may want to do the review early in the week, and then drill it orally a couple of times before giving the test at the end of the week.
- A final comprehensive test is also included.
- Vocabulary Terms and Comprehension Questions with an asterisk in the *Teacher Guide* indicate important plot points that will appear on the quizzes and tests.

Reading Notes

ice box — a refrigerator; originally an insulated chest into which ice was placed to cool and preserve food

Musteline Mammal — a fur-bearing mammal, known for the foul-smelling, oily liquid they eject when frightened or in danger

Genus Mephitis — the Latin name for this family of mammals

Vocabulary

1. He decided to name the skunk **Aroma**. scent
2. That's the last wire **soldered** and my new radio is finished. attached with hot metal
3. The after shave lotion with the **distinctive** invigorating smell *one-of-a-kind
4. The after shave lotion with the distinctive **invigorating** smell energizing
5. so he decided to sneak up and **investigate.** to examine carefully
6. who had evidently gone to college and studied **zoology.** the study of animal life

Comprehension Questions

1. Where does Homer live?

   Homer lives two miles outside of Centerburg, at the intersection of routes 56 and 56A.

2. What exciting news does Homer hear on his new radio?

   A local man had won a slogan contest.

3. Describe the suitcase used to hold the prize money and lotion. Why is this important to note?

   It was just like the suitcase that Homer had at home, where Aroma likes to take naps. Later, Aroma sees this suitcase in the robber's hotel room, and because it looks familiar, he climbs into it.

4. Instead of being a happy celebration, the event becomes frightening. Why?

Four men rob the winner of his prize money and after shave lotion.

5. Why does Homer want to help N. W. Blott get his prize back?

Homer wants to get the reward, so he can build more radios and a television receiver.

Quotations

When Homer isn't going to school, or doing odd jobs, or playing with other boys, he works on his hobby which is building radios. He has a workshop in one corner of his room where he works in the evenings.

Discussion Questions

1. *Using the quotation above, describe Homer. Give reasons for your answers.
2. Why is "Aroma" an appropriate name for Homer's pet skunk?
3. Briefly explain the classification system of the animal kingdom and the role Latin plays in it.

Enrichment

Focus Passage: Copy the fourth full paragraph on page 18 (beginning *"That, my dear friend …"*). Focus on correct spelling, punctuation, and capitalization.

Reading Notes

"I'll be switched."	an idiom meaning "I'm surprised!" or "I can't believe it!"
light button	a light switch
four dollars "in advance"	to pay a price before receiving an item or a service

Vocabulary

1. tried to **coax** Aroma out of the suitcase *tempt
2. Our present condition could be described as being a **trifle** overcrowded. a tiny bit
3. The robbers **gingerly** lifted the covers and peeked out carefully
4. robbers aren't **accustomed** to going without shoes *used to; familiar with
5. the news **commentators** on the radio told about it too. announcers

Comprehension Questions

1. Why do the robbers decide not to shoot Aroma in their hideout in the woods?
   They don't want to attract the sheriff's attention.
2. How does Homer figure out that the four guests at the tourist camp are the robbers?
   The money they give him smells like both after shave lotion and skunk scent.
3. Why does the sheriff wait to arrest the robbers at the tourist camp?
   He is getting his hair cut, and wants to wait until they are asleep.
4. What does the sheriff mean when he says, "the boys and me can walk right in and snap the bracelets on 'em"? He means "put handcuffs on them."
5. Describe Homer's plan to catch the robbers. Who else plays an important part in this plan?
   He watches them through the cabin window. When they talk about going to Mexico, he places Aroma in the room so that the robbers are afraid to move. As they get restless, Homer collects their guns, clothes, and shoes into a basket and marches them down to the sheriff. Aroma plays an important part because of his offensive scent.

Quotations

While they were arguing Homer thought very hard. He guessed that something had better be done pretty quick or the robbers might decide to go before the sheriff got his hair cut. He thought of a plan, and without making a sound, he slipped away from the window and hurried to Aroma's hole under the house.

Discussion Questions

1. Find on page 20, "the air was filled with Aroma!" What is the double meaning of this phrase?
2. Do you agree with Homer's decision not to tell his mother about Aroma? Why or why not?
3. Note the picture of the robbers in bed on p. 25. Do you see anything amiss?

Enrichment

Noticing Details: Look for the answers to the following questions in Chapter 1 of *Homer Price*.

1. What kind of business does Homer's father own? He owns a tourist camp.
2. What is Homer's hobby? He enjoys building radios.
3. What is Homer's cat's name? The cat is named Tabby.
4. Where does Aroma live? Aroma lives under the house right beneath Homer's window.
5. How does Homer tame Aroma? He takes a saucer of milk out to Aroma every evening.
6. What is the name of the person who won the slogan contest? N. W. Blott won the contest.
7. How many guns does Homer think the robbers had in their room? He sees "a dozen or two" guns.
8. Why do the robbers decide to all sleep in the same bed? If one of them gets out of bed (to sneak away with the money), it will surely wake the others up.
9. To what country do the robbers plan to drive? They discuss driving to Mexico.
10. What was Homer's reward for catching the robbers? Homer was allowed to keep Aroma.

Reading Notes

pitch horse shoes a game in which players toss horse shoes at a stake

mail-order house a catalogue company

Vocabulary

1. where the **villain** had put him *criminal
2. [He changes clothes like that] because he is so **modest**. bashful; shy
3. the villain, who turned out to be a very **notorious** criminal. *famously bad
4. with **chromium** trimmings shiny, decorative
5. the Super-Duper's **monogram** on the side. symbol; initials

Comprehension Questions

1. Why is Homer less impressed with the Super-Duper comics than Freddy?

   *He thinks the stories are all too similar. The hero always breaks things up; then he rescues the pretty girl and gets the villain in the end.

2. How does Homer explain the incredible feats of the hero in the movies?

   He says he has learned that they use trick photography.

3. Who are Freddy and Louis, and why are they heading into town?

   Freddy is Homer's friend, and Louis is Freddy's little brother. They are going to pick up a package for their mother.

4. Describe the Super-Duper's car.

   His car is red, chrome-trimmed, stream-lined, and has a monogram.

5. What is the name of the movie the boys see? What happens in the film?

   The movie is called *The Super-Duper and the Electric Ray*. The hero smashes everything and rescues the pretty girl. But the villain gets away so there can be a movie sequel.

Quotations

"Yeh, but it's only a story," said Homer. "And the story's always the same. The Super-Duper always hits things and breaks them up, and a villain always tries to bomb him, or shoot him with a cannon or a gun or an electric ray. Then he always rescues the pretty girl and gets the villain in the end."

Discussion Questions

1. What is the Super-Duper's reason for not flying or bending horse shoes? Do you think that is the real reason? Why not?
2. Does the Super-Duper remind you of a well-known comic hero? Who is it? Give evidence from the story of the similarities between Super-Duper and this hero.

Enrichment

Focus Passage: Copy the conversation between Homer and Freddy beginning on page 37. (Begin with *"Gosh, Freddy ..."* and end on the next page with "Let's go pitch horse shoes.")

Remember to begin a new paragraph with each new quotation. Focus on correct spelling, punctuation, and capitalization.

Reading Notes

barbed-wire fence twisted strands of fence wire with sharp barbs at regular intervals

iodine a liquid used as an antiseptic for wounds

Vocabulary

1. "Golly," said Freddy in a **quavery** voice *wavering; shaky
2. Homer tried hard to make it sound **convincing**. believable
3. and then, the **incredible** happened. unbelievable
4. that same Super-Duper who **defied** the elements *challenged
5. He made faces, just like anybody else, when it was **daubed** on. spread; smeared

Comprehension Questions

1. What happens to the Super-Duper as he leaves the cinema?
   He crashes his car into a ditch.
2. How do Freddy and Louis expect the Super-Duper to get himself out of trouble?
   They expect him to lift his car out of the ditch.
3. How did the Super-Duper end up in the ditch?
   He dodged a skunk as he was rounding a curve in the road.
4. How do the boys help the Super-Duper?
   They hitch Lucy to his car and pull him from the ditch. Then they tow him to Homer's father's garage.
5. What surprises the boys most about the scene?
   They can hardly believe that the Super-Duper feels pain and shows it.

Quotations

The Super-Duper didn't lift the car, no, not yet. He looked at the dent that a fence post had made in his shiny red fender, and then, *the incredible happened. That colossal-osal, gigantic-antic, Super-Duper, that same Super-Duper who defied the elements, who was so strong that he broke up battleships like toothpicks, who was so tough that cannon-balls bounced off his chest, yes, who was* tougher *than steel, he stooped down and said … "Ouch!"*

Discussion Question

As the boys first see the car in the ditch from a distance, do you think Homer is completely convinced that the Super-Duper was not hit by an electric ray? Find the words in the story that support your answer.

Enrichment

Create your own comic strip: Think of four short sentences that summarize the entire sequence of events in Chapter 2, and write them on the lines below. Use the words "first," "next," "then," and "finally" to help you.

Then, find the comic strip illustration page in the Appendix and draw a picture to go with each of the sentences you wrote. Use as much detail as possible in your illustrations.

1. First, First, Homer, Freddy, and Louis are looking at the Super-Duper comic strip.

2. Next, Next, the boys go to the movie and meet the Super-Duper in person.

3. Then, Then, they see the Super-Duper and his car in the ditch.

4. Finally, Finally, they tow the car to the service station, and the Super-Duper gives them comic books.

Reading Notes

Red Cross	an international organization that cares for the wounded and sick in wartime and following natural disasters
receipt	an old word for a recipe
pinochle	a type of card game
tarnation	an expression used to show anger or annoyance

Vocabulary

1. a weakness for labor saving **devices**. *machines
2. Sometimes she became **unkindly disposed** toward him cross; irritated
3. Uncle Ulysses just **frittered away** his spare time wasted
4. a **chauffeur** helped a lady out of the rear door a paid driver
5. it rolled neatly down a little **chute** slide

Comprehension Questions

1. Describe Uncle Ulysses.

   Uncle Ulysses is a man with advanced ideas and a weakness for labor-saving devices. He and his wife own a lunch room in Centerburg.

2. Mr. Gabby describes himself as "a sandwich man." In what way is he like a sandwich?

   His business is in advertising. He travels, walking outdoors, wearing a sign. The sign consists of a board on his front and one on his back, like a human sandwich.

3. In addition to Mr. Gabby, who else visits the lunch room? Describe her.

   A wealthy lady arrives in a black, shiny car (a limousine). She wears a fur coat and lots of jewelry. She also has a chauffeur, named Charles.

4. What concerns Homer about making the doughnuts with Mr. Gabby and the lady?

   Homer is afraid they are mixing too much batter.

5. How does the task go wrong? How many doughnuts does Mr. Gabby count?

   The doughnut machine won't turn off. Mr. Gabby counts 1,202 doughnuts.

Quotations

Homer pushed the button marked "Stop" *and there was a little click, but nothing happened. The rings of batter kept right on dropping into the hot fat, and an automatic gadget kept right on turning them over, and another automatic gadget kept right on giving them a little push and the doughnuts kept right on rolling down the little chute, all ready to eat.*

Discussion Questions

1. Reread the quotation above. Where else do you notice these words in the story? Why do you think the author repeats them so many times?
2. Uncle Ulysses is a huge fan of labor-saving devices. List some common labor-saving devices we use today. Choose one that you think is the most helpful, and support your choice by explaining how this device makes your life easier.
3. The author of this book likes to have fun choosing the names of his characters. Note the names of Homer's aunt and uncle. Why are they interesting? How does Mr. Gabby's name fit his personality?

Enrichment

Focus passage: Copy the complete first paragraph on page 59 (beginning with *"'Yes,' said Homer."*).

Be careful not to lose your place as you copy all the repeating words. Focus on correct spelling, punctuation, and capitalization.

Reading Notes

create the market
supply and demand
merchandising

these are all business terms having to do with buying and selling items

Vocabulary

1. the lunch room was a **calamity** of doughnuts! *disaster
2. You got the doughnuts, ya gotta **create the market**. make buyers desire a product
3. It's **balancing the demand with the supply**. providing the amount buyers want
4. the sheriff cast a **suspicious** eye on Mr. Gabby *distrustful
5. Neatest trick of **merchandising** I ever seen. selling; advertising
6. Aunt Aggy was looking **sceptical*** doubtful

*NOTE: Standard U.S. spelling is *skeptical*.

Comprehension Questions

1. As the doughnut crisis grows, what are Uncle Ulysses' concerns?

   He worries about the amount of unsold doughnuts, the response of his wife, Aggy, and the mess.

2. What does Mr. Gabby suggest to help sell all the extra doughnuts?

   He thinks advertising will help. He suggests they first help people to desire the doughnuts (create the market), which he hopes will create a large demand for them, and then all the doughnuts will be sold.

3. What happens during the doughnut crisis that adds to the day's worries?

   The wealthy lady returns to say that she lost her diamond bracelet while making the dough.

4. Why do people begin helping to solve the problem? A $100 reward is offered for finding the bracelet, and the sign says it will be found in one of the doughnuts.

5. Who finds the missing bracelet? Rupert Black finds the bracelet.

Quotations

Before twenty more doughnuts could roll down the little chute he shouted, "SAY! I know where the bracelet is! It was lying here on the counter and got mixed up in the batter by mistake! The bracelet is cooked inside one of these doughnuts!"

Who said this? Homer

Discussion Questions

1. *How does Homer provide both the cause and the solution to the doughnut problem?
2. Think of a worthwhile item for which you would like to create a market (i.e., cause people to desire it more). Discuss ways in which you could do this.
3. What does Uncle Ulysses say right after he walks into the lunch room and sees the doughnut mess? How does his response add humor to the story? What is that kind of humor called?

Enrichment

Quotation Review: How good is your memory? Supply the name of the speaker for each quotation below. Quotations are taken from Chapters 1-3.

Speaker		Quotation
robber	1.	*"That, my dear friend, is* not *a thing. It is a Musteline Mammal."*
sheriff	2.	*"Yep! that was sure one smell job of swelling."*
Super-Duper	3.	*"I'm sorry, boys, but I haven't time today."*
wealthy lady	4.	*"I haven't had so much fun in years. I* really *haven't!"*
Aunt Agnes	5.	*"My, how that boy does grow!"*
Homer	6.	*"Yeh, but it's only a story. And the story's always the same."*
Rupert Black	7.	*"I GAWT IT!!"*
Freddy	8.	*"He's an awful modest fellow."*
Uncle Ulysses	9.	*"Well, I'll be dunked!!"*
Mr. Gabby	10.	*"A traveling man in outdoor advertising. I'm a sandwich man."*

Character: ***Who** is in the story*

1. Who is the main character in this book? How would you describe him?

Homer Price. He is an average boy who is skilled at solving problems using common sense. He likes to help people and enjoys doing the same things that other boys enjoy. He enjoys building radios.

2. List five other characters from Chapters 1-3.

Answers may include: the four robbers, the sheriff, Mr. Dreggs, Uncle Ulysses, Aunt Agnes, Homer's parents, Aroma, Freddy, little Louis, Super-Duper, Mr. Gabby, the wealthy woman, Charles, or Rupert Black.

Setting: ***Time** and **place** in which the story happens*

1. What is the setting of *Homer Price*?

The setting of *Homer Price* is in the small town of Centerburg. Some of it takes place at Homer's house, where route 56 meets route 56A.

2. List some ways in which life in the story is different from your own.

Possible answers: Cash reward money is put into a suitcase, horse and carriage transportation, children are free and safe to go many places on their own, mail-order packages must be picked up at the station rather than delivered to your house, Homer "gave" the number to the phone operator.

Plot: ***Action** or **what happens** in the story*

Sequence the following events from Chapter 1 in the order in which they happened.

3 Homer and Aroma find the hideout of the robbers, and Aroma adds his scent to the money.

6 Homer gathers the robbers' clothes and guns, and marches them to the sheriff.

4 When the robbers rent a cabin, Homer recognizes them and reports them to the sheriff.

1 Homer finds and tames a skunk, named Aroma, to be his pet.

5 Aroma is sent into the cabin and frightens the robbers into staying awhile.

2 The award money and lotion from Mr. Dreggs' advertising contest are stolen by four robbers.

Character Identification

Write the name of the character on the line next to the description.

1. Freddy is convinced the Super-Duper is a very modest fellow
2. Mr. Gabby a traveling salesman, a “sandwich” man
3. Uncle Ulysses has a weakness for labor-saving devices
4. Super-Duper wrecked his car when he dodged a skunk
5. Homer’s parents own and run a tourist camp and service station
6. wealthy lady has a chauffeur named Charles
7. Aunt Agnes impressed with how fast Homer is growing
8. Homer Price solves problems using common sense
9. Aroma Homer’s pet skunk
10. sheriff often mixes up his words

Illustration

Illustrate Homer Price in your favorite setting from Chapters 1-3.

Quiz I Review

VOCABULARY: Write the letter of the vocabulary word on the line next to its definition.

E 1. machines
C 2. famously bad
J 3. criminal
G 4. distrustful
A 5. one-of-a-kind
I 6. tempt
F 7. disaster
B 8. used to; familar with
H 9. challenged
D 10. wavering; shaky
Q 11. cross; aggravated
M 12. carefully
S 13. doubtful
K 14. scent
N 15. symbol; initials
P 16. slide
T 17. a tiny bit
L 18. the study of animal life
R 19. wasted
O 20. spread; smeared

A. distinctive
B. accustomed
C. notorious
D. quavery
E. devices
F. calamity
G. suspicious
H. defied
I. coax
J. villain
K. aroma
L. zoology
M. gingerly
N. monogram
O. daubed
P. chute
Q. unkindly disposed
R. frittered away
S. sceptical
T. trifle

SHORT ANSWER: Answer the following questions in complete sentences.

1. Describe Homer Price, the main character of this story.

   *Homer Price is a boy who can solve problems using common sense. He works doing odd jobs at his parents' tourist camp, he plays with other boys, and he enjoys building radios as a hobby.

2. What is Homer's opinion about comics in general, and the Super-Duper?

   *He is not impressed because he thinks the stories are all too similar, and he realizes that the Super-Duper is just an ordinary man.

3. How does Homer's common sense help him solve the mystery of the missing bracelet?

   *He calmly thinks back to where the bracelet was while they were mixing the doughnut batter, and when it disappeared. This helps him realize it was accidently mixed into the batter.

QUOTATION IDENTIFICATION: Write the name of the speaker on the line next to each quotation.

1. the wealthy woman — "Just *wait* till you taste these doughnuts!"
2. Homer — "SAY! I know where the bracelet is!"
3. Freddy — "Naaw! Nothing can hurt the Super-Duper because he's too tough."
4. Homer's mother — "We will have to get rid of that animal right away ..."
5. the sheriff — "Well, I'll be switched."
6. Uncle Ulysses — "We must get rid of these doughnuts before Aggy gets here!"
7. Homer — "A real radio broadcast from Centerburg! I'll have to see that!"
8. the Super-Duper — "I didn't want to hit him and get this new car all smelled up."
9. Mr. Gabby — "I lost count at twelve hundred and two and that was quite a while back."
10. (educated) robber — "Our present condition could be described as being a trifle overcrowded."

Reading Notes

rheumatism a condition of the joints and muscles that causes bodily aches and pains

drive a hard bargain to require tough conditions before coming to an agreement with a person

clinch the bargain refers to an action that brings final, solid agreement between two people

Vocabulary

1. Miss Terwilliger is … an **accomplished** knitter highly skilled
2. he would make an **ideal** husband for some fine woman *perfect
3. provide the **diversion** that the trotting races have distraction or entertainment
4. I **appeal** to your sense of county pride. make an earnest request
5. Do not **spurn** the offer. turn down; decline
6. an assistant to help with the **maneuvering** of his ball of string. changing movement or direction

Comprehension Questions

1. Describe Miss Terwilliger. What is unusual about her? She teaches others how to knit and cook. She wears the same blue dress for all special occasions.
2. Why does Aunt Aggy think it would be difficult for a woman to put up with Uncle Telly? She thinks his collecting string is an odd hobby.
3. What does Judge Shank suggest as an alternative to the races for the fair? He suggests a string-measuring contest between Uncle Telly and the sheriff.
4. On what condition do Uncle Telly and the sheriff agree to Judge Shank's suggestion? They agree, as long as the winner gets all of Miss Terwilliger's attention.
5. Describe the rules of the contest. Each contestant is allowed an assistant; the string is to be unwound counter-clockwise around the track two hours each day; the person with the longest string will win the contest.

Quotations

Homer's Uncle Telly lived all by himself in a trim little house near the railroad. Homer's mother always said, "It's a shame that Uncle Telly had to live alone because he would make an ideal husband for some fine woman like Miss 'T'." Aunt Aggy would always answer, "But I don't know how any fine woman could put up with his carryings on!"

Discussion Questions

1. Burning leaves reminds Homer and the sheriff of other things that commonly occur in the fall. What are these fall events? Can you think of others not mentioned?
2. We've already seen that the author likes to have fun with the names of his characters. Can you name four characters found in Greek literature or Greek mythology from which the author has drawn names for the characters of this book? Discuss these characters briefly.

Enrichment

Focus Passage: Copy the last full paragraph on page 78 (beginning with *"Uhumpf! Prize or no prize …"*).

Be careful to copy all quotation marks accurately. Focus on correct spelling, punctuation, and capitalization.

Reading Notes

double cross — to betray someone by violating a prior agreement

parasol — a small, light umbrella carried as protection from the sun

watch like a hawk — to watch someone very carefully (hawks are known for their good vision)

all's fair in love — means there are no "rules" when one is trying to gain the love of another

Vocabulary

1. He was multiplying 3.1416 by the **diameter** the distance across a circle
2. "Do you think," said the sheriff … winking **frantically** *rapidly, with nervous activity
3. the county fair will be an **unprecedented** success. *never before seen
4. each **accused** the other of telling about the agreement. charged; blamed
5. the sheriff **trudged** up and congratulated Miss Terwilliger walked wearily
6. I guess they're the **undisputed** champions now. unarguable

Comprehension Questions

1. Who is the new contestant in the contest? Why is this surprising?
   *Miss Terwilliger is the new contestant. This is surprising because she is also the "prize."
2. What phrase is repeated three times at the beginning of the chapter and, again, four times at the end?
   The phrase "robin's-egg blue" is repeated.
3. As the story reports the progress of Miss Terwilliger around the track, it also describes her clothing. Describe her blue dress at each point.
   First, she is wearing her robin's-egg blue **dress** with the pink trim at the bottom.
   Then, she is wearing her robin's-egg blue **blouse** with a pink skirt.
   Finally, she is wearing her dress with the robin's-egg blue **trim** at the neck and sleeves.
4. How do you think Miss Terwilliger won the contest?
   *She unraveled her blue dress as she needed more yarn to win the contest.
5. Despite losing the String Saver contest, Uncle Telly wins big. Explain.
   Uncle Telly gets married to Miss Terwilliger. He wins the real "prize" he wanted.

Quotations

Practically every woman who was there that day knew how the clever Miss Terwilliger had won the championship. They enjoyed it immensely and laughed among themselves, but they didn't give away the secret because they thought, "all's fair in love," and besides a woman ought to be allowed to make up her own mind.

Discussion Questions

1. When Miss Terwilliger says she wants to enter the contest, the judge says, "The American female is beginning to find her rightful place in the business and public life of this nation." He is said to have made a "fancy speech about 'woman's rights.'" To what are these sentences referring?
2. Where in the United States is Niagara Falls? For what is it known? Find it on a map.

Enrichment

Studying Context Clues: An author often provides written clues to prepare the reader for what will happen later in the story. One way to do this is to repeat lines or phrases he wants the reader to notice. A careful reader will look for these clues to gain deeper understanding and enjoyment of the story. Look for context clues in Chapter 4 of *Homer Price* by answering the questions below.

1. The best example of repetition is the phrase "robin's-egg blue." Where is it repeated, and how does this add to the story? It is repeated three times on page 73 and four times on pages 87-88. It helps us notice that her dress is slowly disappearing as she walks around the track. We laugh at her trick.
2. Find four places where we are told the same information about Miss Terwilliger. How does this offer a clue to her participation in the contest? Pages 73, 79, 82, and 89 all mention that she is "very clever." This hints that she will somehow be involved in the contest and will avoid marrying merely as a result of the men's agreement.
3. Which page reveals a clue that Uncle Telly will indeed marry Miss Terwilliger? Page 74: Homer's mother states that Uncle Telly "would make an ideal husband for … Miss 'T'."
4. Besides what we know about Miss Terwilliger, we are given a clue about yarn that hints at how she wins the contest later on. Can you find it? On page 83 we are told that "yarn stretches."
5. What phrase about men is repeated? How does it help explain the end of the story? "[Men] can hardly tell one dress or suit from another." Uncle Telly and the sheriff don't notice anything unusual about the blue dress and can't figure out that they were tricked in the contest.

Reading Notes

blue plate special	a main course of a restaurant meal, offered at a special price
gaiters	a cloth or leather covering for the leg, from the instep to the ankle or knee
Rip Van Winkle	a story character who sleeps 100 years, then returns from the hills to society
almanac	an annual publication composed of lists, charts, and other general information

Vocabulary

1. conversation had already **dwindled** to nothing at all. became gradually less
2. if I bring you a new customer I get a **commission**. fee
3. he might be a **fugitive** in disguise escaped criminal
4. or maybe one of these **amnesia** cases *memory loss
5. how clever the sheriff was at **deducing** things. reaching a conclusion by reasoning
6. not exactly, a **hermit** … first time he saw people for thirty years. *one who lives alone

Comprehension Questions

1. Why are the men in the barber shop especially interested in the stranger that comes to town?
   They notice his unusual antique car, but they are amazed at his long hair and beard.
2. Why is the sheriff uneasy about the stranger? How does Homer help the sheriff?
   The sheriff doesn't know his intentions. Since the stranger is not shy with children, Homer is able to get information about him to report to the sheriff.
3. What is the stranger's nickname? How does he get this name? "Old Rip";
   Many townspeople tell the sheriff the stranger reminds them of a character in a story. The sheriff goes to the library and decides that the stranger is just like Rip Van Winkle.
4. What does Homer learn about the stranger? Homer learns his real name is Michael Murphy, he has been living in the hills for 30 years, he has invented a special mouse trap, and he wants to rid Centerburg of all its mice.
5. What makes Mr. Murphy's mouse trap so unique?
   It doesn't hurt the mice, it is huge, and it uses music as bait.

Quotations

It wasn't because this car was old, old enough to be an antique; or because some strange business was built onto it; or that the strange business was covered with a large canvas. No, that wasn't what made Homer and the sheriff, and Uncle Ulysses, and the barber stare so long. It was the car's driver.

Discussion Questions

1. After his first impressions, how does the sheriff describe the stranger? Why is this humorous?
2. Contrast the information people in the story use to "judge" others. What conclusion can you draw?
3. Homer says Mr. Murphy read that "if a man can make a better mouse trap than anybody else, the world will beat a path to his house." What does this mean? What is the double meaning here?

Enrichment

Focus Passage: Copy the last three paragraphs on page 105 (beginning with "Bright and early …" and ending with "… do the finding!").

Be careful to indent new paragraphs and to copy all quotation marks accurately.
Focus on correct spelling, punctuation, and capitalization.

Reading Notes

thing of a jig — a slang term for an unnamed, unknown object

license plate — a metal sign on a car, showing official permission to own and operate

Pied Piper of Hamelin — a story character who charms first mice, and then children, into following him

Vocabulary

1. **painstakingly** arranged the spiral ramps with great care
2. *The **Pied** Piper of Hamelin* *multi-colored
3. Mr. Murphy was very **flustered** agitated; confused
4. The mice came out in a **torrent**. flood
5. That music has **pixied** these children! *put a magic spell on

Comprehension Questions

1. How does Homer's common sense prompt him to be suspicious of the pied piper?
He goes to the library and reads that music can do funny things, such as charm wild animals.

2. How much is Mr. Murphy's fee for removing mice? Why isn't he allowed to keep the fee?
He charges 30 dollars, but has to pay the same amount for a new license plate.

3. What does the librarian discover about the stranger? Why is she so upset by it?
She realizes the story of *The Pied Piper of Hamelin* is a better fit for the situation than *Rip Van Winkle*. She knows that in that story the pied piper leads all the children away.

4. How does the sheriff get Mr. Murphy to release the children?
He drives next to his car, pays him 30 dollars more, and orders him to "Let 'em go."

5. How does Mr. Murphy misunderstand the sheriff, and what happens as a result?
Mr. Murphy thinks the sheriff wants him to release all the mice, so he does, and they all return to Centerburg.

6. In what way does Homer's cleverness protect the children from possible danger?
Homer asks the doctor to put cotton in their ears so they can't hear the charming music.

Quotations

There's no telling how this de-mousing would have ended if the children's librarian hadn't come rushing up shouting "Sheriff! Sheriff! Quick! We guessed the wrong book! *... Yes!" gasped the children's librarian, "not* Rip Van Winkle, *but* another *book,* The Pied Piper of Hamelin*!"*

Discussion Questions

1. You have learned to be watching for context clues in a story that foretell coming events. Find a clue on page 113 that hints at coming trouble.

Enrichment

DRAWING COMPARISONS AND CONTRASTS:

Read the story *Rip Van Winkle* (found in the Appendix of this guide).
Compare and contrast this story with Chapter 5 of *Homer Price*, using the chart on the following page.

What is the moral of the story *Rip Van Winkle*?

The moral might be "don't be lazy"; in this case, if you are lazy you will miss out on life.

Read the story *The Pied Piper of Hamelin* (found in the Appendix of this guide).

Compare and contrast this story with Chapter 5 of *Homer Price*, using the chart on the following page.

What is the moral of the story *The Pied Piper of Hamelin*?

The moral might be "keep your promises"; in this case, pay the money you have promised to pay.

Read the story of Odysseus (can be found in *Famous Men of Greece*, Memoria Press).

How is the ancient story of Odysseus similar to *Homer Price*, Chapter 5?

Odysseus (or Roman, Ulysses) plugs the ears of his sailors so they can't hear the "charming" call of the Sirens as they sail past. Homer plugs the ears of the children so they can't hear the music.

Rip Van Winkle

List the ways in which Mr. Murphy is **similar** to Rip Van Winkle in this chapter.

List the ways in which Mr. Murphy is **different** from Rip Van Winkle in this chapter.

Illustrate your favorite portion of *Rip Van Winkle* below:

The Pied Piper of Hamelin

List the ways in which Mr. Murphy is **similar** to the Pied Piper in this chapter.

List the ways in which Mr. Murphy is **different** from the Pied Piper in this chapter.

Illustrate your favorite portion of *The Pied Piper of Hamelin* below:

Reading Notes

too many cooks spoil the soup	too many workers at the same job can get in each other's way
pet theories	favorite ideas or beliefs
landscape architect	someone who plans beautiful gardens around houses
era	a period of time characterized by particular circumstances

Vocabulary

1. Because it isn't **imperative** that I hafta go fishing. *absolutely necessary
2. help me adjust the timing **mechanism** in this toaster. working parts
3. she has a **receptive** mind receiving; willing to consider change
4. they could be **replicas** of the Enders homestead *copies; models
5. That's the **principle**! main idea; belief
6. and a touch of **ingenuity** cleverness; inventiveness

Comprehension Questions

1. Who is Miss Enders? How did she come to live in Centerburg?
   She is the great-great-great-granddaughter of Ezekiel Enders, the first settler of Centerburg. She recently inherited all the Enders property and now lives in the Enders Homestead at the edge of town.
2. Why does Uncle Ulysses think so highly of Miss Enders?
   He is pleased that she is receptive to new devices and modern methods.
3. What plan does Miss Enders propose to help the housing shortage?
   She offers to donate some of her property in order to develop new housing.
4. Why does this project excite Uncle Ulysses?
   He is excited about new devices and methods; he sees how mass production and assembly lines can help a business.
5. How does the project change, and what is the reasoning behind this change?
   More houses are built than was planned because Uncle Ulysses thinks building more makes all the work and trouble worthwhile.

Quotations

"That's the principle that Henry Ford applied to making autos. Yep! Autos are mass produced, like doughnuts; ships are built like doughnuts; airplanes and refrigerators, and now houses. *Yessiree, the* modern *house ought to be mass produced—just like cars or ships or planes. Yessiree!"*

Who said this? Uncle Ulysses To whom is he speaking? Homer and Miss Enders

Discussion Questions

1. Who was Henry Ford and where did he live? For what is he famous? How does Uncle Ulysses explain the benefits of mass production and assembly lines?
2. At the end of this section of the chapter, Miss Enders says, "Just think. Last week there were only grass and trees and squirrels on this spot!" Do you think the author is suggesting that this is a good change or a bad one? What do you think?

Enrichment

Focus Passage: Copy the fifth full paragraph on page 129 (beginning with *"That's the principle ..."* and ending with *"Snap!"*).

Watch for the quotation marks and copy them accurately. Focus on correct spelling, punctuation, and capitalization.

Reading Notes

Whistler's Mother	a famous painting by James McNeill Whistler
proud as Punch	from the famous puppets Punch and Judy; Punch is proud of his wrong deeds
pantomime	to act a part without using words
elixir	a substance believed to maintain life indefinitely

Vocabulary

1. newspaper said in an **editorial** an opinion-based article
2. The union surely wouldn't **object** to that! disapprove of
3. Couldn't you **arbitrate** or something? help settle; decide
4. the union will have to **picket** march in protest
5. found forty-two pounds of **edible fungus** growing safe-to-eat mushrooms
6. the Indian uprising was **quelled** *stopped

Comprehension Questions

1. What is the argument between Uncle Ulysses and Dulcey Dooner?
   The argument is about an acceptable rate for installing street signs.
2. How do the new tenants find their way to their own homes?
   They must count the number of houses away from the Enders Homestead they are located.
3. Who founded the city that is now Centerburg? What was the city's first name?
   Miss Enders' ancestor, Ezekiel Enders, founded the city named Edible Fungus.
4. Why were the street signs not erected after the pageant ended?
   Dulcey Dooner had drunk a cask of the cough syrup, aged over 100 years, and it put him to sleep.
5. How did the Dulcey Dooner incident benefit the city?
   He accidently found the site of the homestead, which provided a way for everyone to find their home once again.

Quotations

Another house, like all the others, stood in its place. One hundred and one houses, all alike, down to the last door knob! Each with its climbing rose bush, two dwarf cedars, and maple tree sodded round about. Just as alike as one hundred and one doughnuts, and nothing, no nothing to count from to find out which was which and whose was whose. There was a mad scramble, with much shouting, with the deserving tenants trying frantically to find out which house was which.

Discussion Questions

1. What items are included in each house in the new suburb? Is this good or bad? Why?
2. What is a "union"? What problem did the Street Sign Putter Uppers Union cause for Centerburg?

Character Identification

Write the name of the speaker on the line next to each quotation.

1. Aunt Agnes ______ *"But I don't know how any fine woman could put up with his carryings on!"*
2. Miss Enders ______ *"It's marvelous, simply marvelous!"*
3. Homer ______ *"It's just to be on the safe side."*
4. Miss Terwilliger ______ *"Isn't it* wonderful *that we have* so *much in common?"*
5. Uncle Ulysses ______ *"Yessiree, the* modern *house ought to be mass produced."*
6. Tony (shoe repair man) ______ *"Well, Sheriff,* I *judge everybody by their* feet, *and their* shoes.*"*
7. the sheriff ______ *"Get 'em low! Get 'em go! Durnit, Let 'em go!"*
8. Dulcey Dooner ______ *"Ya see … I make all the union rules, pay all the dues (and collect them too) so what I say goes."*
9. Uncle Telly ______ *"Wind it tight; don't let anybody say that my string isn't wound right!"*
10. the librarian ______ *"Sheriff! Sheriff! Quick!* We guessed the wrong book!*"*

Character: ***Who*** *is in the story*

1. List the minor characters from Chapters 4-6.

Uncle Ulysses, Uncle Telly, the sheriff, Miss Terwilliger, Aunt Aggy, the judge, the barber, Mr. Murphy, the mayor, the librarian, the town children, Miss Enders, Dulcey Dooner

2. Choose one of the minor characters above, and write a sentence about something they did that you thought was humorous.

Anwers will vary.

Setting: ***Time*** *and* ***place*** *in which the story happens*

Chapters 4-6 are set in the fall season. Using your senses (sight, smell, hearing, taste, touch), write two sentences describing fall.

Anwers will vary.

Plot: ***Action*** *or* ***what happens*** *in the story*

Sequence the following events from Chapter 5 in the order in which they happened.

6 Mr. Murphy misunderstands the sheriff and releases all the mice back into the town.

3 Mr. Murphy agrees to catch all the town mice and drive them out of town to release them.

1 An unusual-looking stranger comes to Centerburg, causing the sheriff to be uneasy.

4 All the town's children follow Mr. Murphy as he collects the mice in his amazing machine.

5 The librarian tells the sheriff "Old Rip" is really more like the Pied Piper, and must be stopped.

2 Homer learns that "Old Rip" has made a special mouse trap and brings him to the mayor.

Character Identification

Write the name of the character on the line next to the description.

1. Dulcey Dooner ______ refuses to put up street signs unless he is paid $10 per sign
2. the barber ______ judges people by their hair
3. the mayor ______ hires the stranger to catch all the town's mice
4. Miss Enders ______ donates some of her property to build a new suburb
5. Uncle Telly ______ thinks Miss Terwilliger is a great cook and wants to marry her
6. the judge ______ wants to cut expenses at the fair by holding a string-saver contest
7. Homer ______ discovers important information by researching books at the library
8. the librarian ______ warns the sheriff that the children of Centerburg may be in danger
9. Miss Terwilliger ______ a very clever woman
10. Uncle Ulysses ______ very enthusiastic about mass production and assembly lines

Illustration

Illustrate Homer Price in your favorite setting from Chapters 4-6.

Quiz 2 Review

VOCABULARY: Write the letter of the vocabulary word on the line next to its definition.

G 1. absolutely necessary
E 2. one who lives alone
I 3. stopped
B 4. rapidly, with nervous activity
J 5. multi-colored
H 6. copies, models
C 7. never before seen
F 8. put a magic spell on
D 9. memory loss
A 10. perfect
N 11. became gradually less
L 12. changing movement or direction
P 13. fee
R 14. agitated; confused
T 15. disapprove of
K 16. turn down; decline
O 17. escaped criminal
S 18. cleverness; inventiveness
M 19. charged; blamed
Q 20. flood

A. ideal
B. frantically
C. unprecedented
D. amnesia
E. hermit
F. pixied
G. imperative
H. replicas
I. quelled
J. pied
K. spurn
L. maneuvering
M. accused
N. dwindled
O. fugitive
P. commission
Q. torrent
R. flustered
S. ingenuity
T. object

SHORT ANSWER: Answer the following questions in complete sentences.

1. What did Miss Terwilliger do that displayed her cleverness?

   *When she suspected she was the "prize" of the contest, she entered it herself and found a way to win. She wore her stretchy, blue yarn dress over another dress and unraveled it as she needed more yarn.

2. What very important difference is there between Mr. Murphy and the Pied Piper at the end of the chapter?

   *Mr. Murphy is only sad about not getting his money; he doesn't disappear with the children as the piper does.

3. Describe one benefit and one harmful effect that occurred in Centerburg as a result of mass production.

   *More houses and modern devices were made available for the people. However, these items were made by a machine and may not be of good quality. There is no interesting variety in this new neighborhood; people have trouble finding their own home.

QUOTATION IDENTIFICATION: Write the name of the speaker on the line in front of each quotation.

1. the librarian "… not *Rip Van Winkle*, but *another* book, *The Pied Piper of Hamelin*!"
2. Dulcey Dooner "Nope, it's ten dollars or nothing."
3. Uncle Telly "That woman certainly can cook!"
4. the mayor "I wondered where my jelly beans were disappearing to!"
5. Miss Terwilliger "I have a beautiful ball of yarn, all colors of the rainbow."
6. the judge "I appeal to your sense of county pride. Do not spurn the offer."
7. Uncle Ulysses "That's the principle!"
8. Homer "This is where Ezekiel buried it! And this is where the Homestead stood!"
9. the sheriff "I think I'll start savin' paper bags or bottle caps!"
10. Miss Enders "I've decided … to build a few homes on the family property."

Vocabulary Crossword

Use your vocabulary knowledge from reading *Homer Price* to complete the following crossword:

Across:

6 multi-colored
9 never before seen
13 perfect
16 one-of-a-kind
17 memory loss
18 challenged
20 famously bad

Down:

1 criminal
2 put a magic spell on
3 used to; familiar with
4 one who lives alone
5 stopped
7 absolutely necessary
8 copies; models
10 disaster
11 distrustful
12 wavering; shaky
14 machines
15 rapidly, w/ nervous activity
19 tempt

WORDBANK

distinctive	ideal
coax	frantically
accustomed	unprecedented
villain	amnesia
notorious	hermit
quavery	pied
defied	pixied
devices	imperative
calamity	replicas
suspicious	quelled

Character Identification

Using the following names, match each name to a description and write the name on the line.

Freddy	Miss Terwilliger	Aroma	the librarian	Homer
Mr. Gabby	the sheriff	Uncle Telly	Uncle Ulysses	Miss Enders

1. Homer solves problems using common sense
2. Aroma Homer's pet skunk
3. Uncle Ulysses has a weakness for labor-saving devices
4. Miss Enders donates some of her property to build a new suburb
5. Mr. Gabby a traveling salesman, a "sandwich" man
6. the sheriff often mixes up his words
7. the librarian warns the sheriff that the town's children are in danger
8. Freddy is convinced the Super-Duper is a very modest fellow
9. Uncle Telly thinks Miss Terwilliger is a great cook
10. Miss Terwilliger a very clever woman

Who Said That?

Write the name of the speaker on the line in front of each quotation.

1. the mayor "I wondered where my jelly beans were disappearing to!"
2. Homer "SAY! I know where the bracelet is!"
3. the robber "That, my dear friend, is *not* a thing. It is a Musteline Mammal."
4. Freddy "He's an awful modest fellow."
5. Miss Terwilliger "Isn't it *wonderful* that we have *so* much in common?"
6. Aunt Agnes "My, how that boy does grow!"
7. Mr. Gabby "A traveling man in outdoor advertising. I'm a sandwich man."
8. Dulcey Dooner "Nope, it's ten dollars or nothing."
9. Uncle Ulysses "Well, I'll be dunked!!"
10. Miss Enders "It's marvelous, simply marvelous!"

Ordering Events

Number the events of each chapter in the order in which they occurred.

Chapter 1

4 When the robbers rent a cabin, Homer recognizes them and reports them to the sheriff.

6 Homer gathers the robbers' clothes and guns, and marches them to the sheriff.

2 The award money and lotion from Mr. Dreggs' advertising contest are stolen by four robbers.

5 Aroma is sent into the cabin and frightens the robbers into staying awhile.

3 Homer and Aroma find the hideout of the robbers, and Aroma adds his scent to the money.

1 Homer finds and tames a skunk, named Aroma, to be his pet.

Chapter 2

4 The Super-Duper wrecks his car trying to avoid a skunk crossing the road.

6 Super-Duper gives the boys a gift of his comic books.

2 The boys meet Super-Duper at the theater, where he refuses to fly for them.

5 The boys pull the car out of the ditch and tow it to Homer's father's garage.

1 Homer, Freddy, and Louis look at Super-Duper comic books, but Homer is not impressed.

3 A fast car speeding around the curve passes the boys driving their horse and wagon.

Chapter 3

5 The wealthy woman comes back looking for her lost bracelet.

1 A friendly salesman comes to the lunch room for coffee and doughnuts.

3 The doughnut machine breaks and won't stop producing doughnuts.

6 Homer offers a reward for the bracelet and tells people it will be found in a doughnut.

4 Homer and Mr. Gabby think of a way to sell all the extra doughnuts.

2 A wealthy woman arrives at the lunch room and offers to make her special doughnut batter.

Chapter 4

2 The sheriff and Uncle Telly agree to a String Saving contest at the county fair.

4 Miss Terwilliger surprises everyone and enters the contest herself.

6 Uncle Telly and Miss Terwilliger are married. The sheriff decides to save bottle caps.

3 The men decide that Miss Terwilliger should be the secret "prize" for the contest.

5 Miss Terwilliger wears her blue dress and wins the contest.

1 We meet Miss Terwilliger and learn that both Uncle Telly and the sheriff want to marry her.

Chapter 5

2 Homer learns that "Old Rip" has made a special mouse trap and brings him to the mayor.

3 Mr. Murphy agrees to catch all the town mice and drive them out of town to release them.

5 The librarian tells the sheriff "Old Rip" is really more like the Pied Piper, and must be stopped.

4 All the town's children follow Mr. Murphy as he collects the mice in his amazing machine.

6 Mr. Murphy misunderstands the sheriff and releases all the mice back into the town.

1 An unusual-looking stranger comes to Centerburg, causing the sheriff to be uneasy.

Chapter 6

4 Dulcey Dooner is hired to put in much-needed street signs in the new suburb.

1 Miss Enders lives in Centerburg and offers her property to build a new suburb.

6 Dulcey Dooner finds the buried Cough Syrup & Elixir Compound, and the homestead is rebuilt.

2 Uncle Ulysses is especially interested in mass producing houses and gives lots of advice.

5 The homestead is replaced with a new suburban house, and nobody can find their own home.

3 One hundred identical houses are built surrounding the old Enders Homestead.

Short Answer

Write a phrase or sentence for each question.

1. Describe Homer Price, the main character of this story.

*Homer Price is a boy who can solve problems using common sense. He works doing odd jobs at his parents' tourist camp, he plays with other boys, and he enjoys building radios as a hobby.

2. How does Homer's common sense help him solve the mystery of the missing bracelet?

*He calmly thinks back to where the bracelet was while they were mixing the doughnut batter and when it disappeared. This helps him realize it was accidently mixed into the batter.

3. What did Miss Terwilliger do that displayed her cleverness?

*When she suspected she was the "prize" of the contest, she entered it herself and found a way to win. She wore her stretchy, blue yarn dress over another dress and unraveled it as she needed more yarn.

4. What very important difference is there between Mr. Murphy and the Pied Piper at the end of the chapter?

*Mr. Murphy is only sad about not getting his money; he doesn't disappear with the children as the piper does.

5. Describe one benefit and one harmful effect that occurred in Centerburg as a result of mass production.

*More houses and modern devices were made available for the people. However, these items were made by a machine and may not be of good quality. There is no interesting variety in this new neighborhood; people have trouble finding their own home.

APPENDIX

Biographical Sketch

Robert McCloskey (1914-2003) was born in Hamilton, Ohio. He wrote and illustrated eight books, two of which won the Caldecott Honor award, and two of which were awarded the prestigious Caldecott Medal award.

As a child growing up in a small town in the Midwest, McCloskey's parents encouraged him to pursue his interests. His love for music led him to the piano, harmonica, drums, and oboe. This love, though never abandoned, gave way later to an interest in mechanics and inventing. He tinkered with old electric trains and clocks, and even built a train with a remote control.

In high school, McCloskey's interests took another turn. He was asked to do drawings for his school annual and discovered a talent and strong love for art. This led to a college scholarship to Vesper George Art School in Boston. While in Boston, he often walked through the Public Gardens on his way to school and spent leisure time watching the ducks there. In 1934 he was given his first major art commission, and in 1936 he moved to New York City to study at the National Academy of Design and pursue a professional art career. But McCloskey had trouble selling his paintings with themes of Greek mythology and dragons, and his career never really took off. After eventually visiting a children's book editor, he was encouraged to focus on what he knew best, and in 1938 moved back to the Midwest.

In Ohio, McCloskey once again drew inspiration for his drawings from the small town setting and built up his portfolio. His first book, *Lentil*, was published in 1939; it is about the story of a boy who, when disappointed in his inability to sing, learns to play the harmonica. McCloskey was soon thereafter hired to paint murals in a wealthy Boston suburb, and moved back to the area.

In 1940, McCloskey married Peggy Durand, a children's librarian, who was the daughter of the children's author Ruth Sawyer. The McCloskeys had two children, Sally and Jane.

McCloskey's second and arguably most popular book, *Make Way for Ducklings*, was published in 1942. The story follows a mother duck searching for a suitable place in Boston to raise her young. To gain details for his drawings, he purchased six mallard ducklings, following them in his studio and watching them swim in his bathtub. The pictures came easily, but the writing was more difficult for him. He had to rewrite the book many times before he was satisfied with the end result.

Homer Price, the story of the adventures of a young inventor in the rural Midwest, followed in 1943. He continued this story later in the book *Centerburg Tales*. These books were later translated into Russian in the 1970s and became popular in the USSR.

In the late 1940s, McCloskey and his family moved to an island off the northern coast of Maine. Successive books now reflected his love of the ocean and his family. *Blueberries for Sal* featured his wife and eldest daughter, Sally. *One Morning in Maine* included his younger daughter, Jane. With the publishing of *Time of Wonder*, he became the first author to win two coveted Caldecott Medal awards. His final book, *Burt Dow: Deep-Water Man*, appeared in 1963.

Those who knew Robert McCloskey described him as a modest man concerning his skills as a writer: "It's just sort of an accident that I write books." "I really think up stories in pictures and just fill in between the pictures with a sentence or a paragraph or a few pages of words."

Create Your Own Comic Strip

Rip Van Winkle

by

Washington Irving

(Adapted for younger readers by Dayna Grant)

Nestled in the foot of the Kaatskills mountains near the Hudson River, lies an idyllic village settled by Dutch colonists many years ago. In the years right before the Revolutionary War, there lived in this village a shiftless but most amiable man by the name of Rip Van Winkle. Though a husband and a father and a farmer, he worked very little at being good at any of these things. He preferred instead to work very hard at being pleasantly idle. He could be found flying kites or playing marbles with the village children who dogged his wandering steps, or telling them long stories of ghosts and witches and Indians. You might see him running an unimportant errand for a neighbor, or fishing all day without catching a single fish, or even building a neighborhood fence if it got him away from his own pressing chores at home. More often than not, you would find him lazing about on a bench in front of the village inn with his equally useless friends, gossiping or making wise pronouncements about current events. In short, Rip would happily engage in any activity except that which would be genuinely useful.

His wife was not the kind to be silent in regards to Rip's shortcomings, but her attempts to berate and nag and shame him into being a more useful sort of person failed entirely. After many years of marriage, Rip would often be forced to wander far into the woods to escape his work and his wife. One day he had wandered to the highest part of the Kaatskills mountains with his hunting rifle, and, fearing his wife's rage if he returned too late, had begun to head home when he heard someone calling his name in the distance. As he approached the voice he found a strange man in old-fashioned clothes carrying a heavy cask up the mountain. Always willing to help a neighbor, Rip helped him carry his load up the mountain to his companions.

As they approached the rest of the party, an odd sound, like the long, rolling peals of distant thunder, could be heard. They entered a hidden opening in the mountains where the man's companions, similarly dressed in outdated clothes, were playing a very serious game of bowling. All was quiet except for the echoing sound of thunder coming from the rolling ball. Rip, not one to pass up a party, no matter how strange, passed out drinks from the cask he'd helped carry up the mountain, and drank a few himself. As he drank the strange liquid, he got more and more tired until he finally fell asleep, curled on the ground.

When he awoke in the brightness of morning, his companions had vanished. The shiny hunting rifle he'd placed on the ground beside him the night before appeared to have been replaced with a rusted and rotting rifle. Confused, but knowing his wife's anger increased with every minute he failed to return home, he hurried down into the village. As he wandered through streets that seemed to have transformed overnight, he drew curious gazes and a troop of children, all of them strangely unfamiliar. He reached up to rub his chin in bewilderment, and discovered his beard had grown a foot overnight. And then he started to suspect he had slept longer than one night.

He walked to his house to find it abandoned, his wife and children absent. He walked through streets that were no longer familiar and greeted people in the streets that he didn't know. He walked to the inn to discover one of his friends had died eighteen years ago, one had died in the Revolutionary War which had taken place while he slept, and one was now a member of the Congress of the new United States of America.

Completely at a loss, Rip asked if anyone knew a man named Rip Van Winkle. "Yes!" cried the villagers. "He disappeared," they said, "some twenty years ago. He went into the woods with his hunting rifle and hasn't been seen or heard from since."

This was quite a shock to Rip, who stood before them with ragged clothes and an unruly beard, to find out that he fell asleep one night and slept for twenty years. His wife had died, they told him, and his children were all grown with children of their own.

"But I am Rip!" he cried. "Young Rip Van Winkle once—old Rip Van Winkle now! Does nobody know poor Rip Van Winkle?"

And there was much exclaiming and explaining and consulting. And finally, it was decided that he was, in fact, the very same Rip Van Winkle who had disappeared twenty years ago or yesterday, and that strange things had been known to happen deep in the Kaatskills mountains. The villagers consulted the town historian (that is to say, the oldest man in the village, who was fond of gossip and stories), and learned that Hendrick Hudson, discoverer of the Hudson River and surrounding territories, is said to return every twenty years to keep a watchful eye on his lands. The strange companions in outdated clothing Rip found bowling in the mountains must surely have been Hudson and his crew, and the contents of the cask Rip so enthusiastically drank must have bewitched him.

And while this was all rather shocking, it did not much alter the daily life of Rip Van Winkle. He soon became a favorite playmate of a new generation of children, located those of his idling friends who were still alive, and took up his spot on the bench outside the inn once more. He even became a sort of revered patriarch of the village, a relic of the time "before the war." An old man, Rip found, can be idle with impunity.

The Pied Piper of Hamelin

based on the Robert Browning poem

(Adapted for younger readers by Dayna Grant)

The charming little town of Hamelin in Brunswick, Germany, was beset nearly five hundred years ago by an infestation of rodents. Hundreds and hundreds of rats roamed the streets of Hamelin, fighting with dogs and killing cats and biting babies and ruining food. They created such a ruckus they often drowned out the sound of ladies chatting in the streets.

The townspeople, understandably, did not want these unwelcome guests in their town. The people gathered in the Town Hall and made it clear that a foolish Mayor and useless Town Councilmen who could not rid their town of rats would soon be looking for new jobs. Now, you would have to look long and hard before you found lazier or greedier men than the Mayor and the Councilmen. They very much enjoyed the usually easy and very lucrative job of running the town, so they sat down to search their empty heads for ideas.

After an hour of fruitless thinking, they gave up in despair. At that same moment, a gentle tap was heard at the chamber door, and in walked a tall, clean-shaven, colorfully attired stranger. He told the men that he was able, by means of his pipe and a secret charm, to cause any living creature to follow after him wherever he willed. The man spoke of his exploits ridding other towns of unwelcome pests and vermin, and offered to do the same for Hamelin, for a small price. The Mayor and Councilmen, giddy with relief, told the piper they'd pay him fifty times what he asked, if only he'd rid the town of rats.

The piper stepped into the street and blew three notes on his pipe. A faint rumbling began, growing louder and louder, until rats began to flow out from houses and holes. And all the rats in all the town followed the strange little piper to the river outside the town wall. One by one they all jumped in the river and drowned, except one stout rat who managed to swim across. He went back to Rat-land and told all the rats there about the man who piped three shrill notes on a pipe and made all the rats in Hamelin believe the whole world had been turned into a giant pantry. The rats of Hamelin heard the sounds of corks popping and crackers crunching and the glorious sound of cupboards opening, and they followed those sounds to the bottom of the river.

But in Hamelin, the townspeople rang bells and rejoiced and danced in the square. In the midst of this the piper's voice was heard saying, "But first, if you please, my payment!" And at this the Mayor and Town Council remembered their hasty promise of generous payment, and their greedy little hearts froze with horror. They thought of all the lovely coats and mouth-watering foods they could buy with the money they'd promised the piper and they did not want to pay him.

"You will regret this!" threatened the piper.

"Well," said they, "you've already done what we wanted. You may have a paltry payment for your services, and a drink of course, for we are not ungenerous, but then you must be on your way. For what have we to fear from you? Do your worst!"

To this pronouncement the piper gave no response. He simply stepped out into the street and blew three sweet notes on his pipe. And out of the houses and down the lanes skipped all the children of the town. They hopped and laughed and danced and happily followed the piper where he led. He guided them through the streets and past the river, and straight towards Koppelberg Hill, as the townspeople watched, helpless. And the townspeople thought, perhaps, that the piper and the children would never be able to climb over the mountain and that the children would be returned to them. But as the procession approached, a portal opened in the side of the mountain and the piper marched straight into it, the children following behind. And as the last child (excepting one little boy with a limp who couldn't keep up with the rest) ran through the portal it sealed itself up as if it had never been there.

The townspeople looked everywhere for their lost children, and the Mayor even offered a large reward to anyone who could return them, but they were never seen or heard from again. Though there is a tale, in far away Transylvania, of a strange tribe of people foreign to those lands, whose parents were said to have risen from an underground tunnel, telling remarkable stories of music and mountains and a charming little town called Hamelin.

DISCUSSION QUESTIONS

Answer Key

Chapter I, Part 1:

1. Using the quotation above, describe Homer. Give reasons for your answers.
   **Homer is a normal, average little boy. He goes to school, he helps his parents by doing odd jobs for their business, and he plays with other little boys. But Homer is also evidently an intelligent boy who has the skills to make workable radios for a hobby.*

2. Why is "Aroma" an appropriate name for Homer's pet skunk?
   "Aroma" means "scent." Since Aroma is a skunk and is capable of giving off strong scents when frightened, this is an appropriate name for him.

3. Briefly explain the classification system of the animal kingdom and the role Latin plays in it.
   The scientific classification system is a means of organizing all animals into groups with similar animals. Animals that have backbones are grouped into 5 classes: fish, amphibians, reptiles, birds, and mammals.
   Every plant and animal species was given its own special Latin name. For example, "Canis lupus" is the scientific Latin name for "dog." "Tyrannasaurus Rex" is the name for the largest known dinosaur, the "King."

Chapter I, Part 2:

1. Find on page 20, "the air was filled with Aroma." What is the double meaning of this phrase?
   Literally, it means that the air was filled with the smell of the after shave lotion and the smell of the skunk. The double meaning is that the word "aroma" is another word for a "smell." So the smell of this skunk is the smell or "aroma" of Homer's pet, Aroma!

2. Do you agree with Homer's decision not to tell his mother about Aroma? Why or why not?
   Answers will vary.

3. Note the picture of the robbers in bed on p. 25. Do you see anything amiss?
   The story talks about four robbers. The illustration shows five robbers in the bed with the suitcase.

Chapter II, Part 1:

1. What is the Super-Duper's reason for not flying or bending horse shoes? Do you think that is the real reason? Why not?
   Super-Duper says he has no time to fly or bend horse shoes for the boys. The real reason is that he knows he is a normal man and cannot do those feats of super strength.

2. Does the Super-Duper remind you of a well-known comic hero? Who is it? Give evidence from the story of the similarities between Super-Duper and this hero.
   He reminds us of Superman. Superman does the same feats of super strength as described in the story. Superman also dresses similar to Super-Duper, in red and blue, as seen in the illustration on page 40.

Chapter II, Part 2:

1. As the boys first see the car in the ditch from a distance, do you think Homer is completely convinced that the Super-Duper was not hit by an electric ray? Find the words in the story that support your answer.

   No, Homer is not completely convinced that "the electric ray business was just part of a movie." When he answers Louis, Homer speaks in his "bravest voice." Also, when he is trying to comfort Louis, Homer "tried hard to make it sound convincing." He was also trying to convince himself!

Chapter III, Part 1:

1. Reread the quotation above. Where else do you notice these words in the story? Why do you think the author repeats them so many times?

   This paragraph is also found on page 56, when Homer pushes the "Start" button on the machine. It occurs again on the top of page 58, after he tries to turn off the machine, and once again on the top of page 59, when he is leaving a message for his uncle with the sheriff. (It repeats again in Part 2, on page 63, as they paint the "Sale on Doughnuts" signs, and again at the very end of the chapter, spoken by Uncle Ulysses.) The repetition of these words draws your attention to them and adds interest to the story. The words themselves sound like a machine that won't stop producing something (i.e., "kept right on" ...).

2. Uncle Ulysess is a huge fan of labor-saving devices. List some common labor-saving devices we use today. Choose one that you think is the most helpful, and support your choice by explaining how this device makes your life easier.

   Answers will vary.

3. The author of this book likes to have fun choosing the names of his characters. Note the names of Homer's aunt and uncle. Why are they interesting? How does Mr. Gabby's name fit his personality?

   Uncle Ulysses and Aunt Agnus are interesting because they are formed using alliteration (the intentional repetition of the same sound in a series of words). Mr. Gabby's name fits his personality because he is a salesman, and they typically do much talking, or "gabbing." This is true of Mr. Gabby in the story.

Chapter III, Part 2:

1. How does Homer provide both the cause and the solution to the doughnut problem?

   **Homer is the one who put the missing pieces back into the machine. He probably put them in the wrong place, causing the machine to malfunction. When Mr. Gabby mentions advertising, Homer suggests the plan that he wear a sign advertising doughnuts. Homer also has the idea to make a new sign offering a reward for the bracelet, while also telling the people that the bracelet will be found inside one of the doughnuts.*

2. Think of a worthwhile item for which you would like to create a market (i.e., cause people to desire it more). Discuss ways in which you could do this.

   Answers will vary.

3. What does Uncle Ulysses say right after he walks into the lunch room and sees the doughtnut mess? How does his response add humor to the story? What is that kind of humor called?

   Uncle Ulysses says, "Well, I'll be dunked!!" This response adds humor to the story because it has a double meaning; the story is about doughnuts, which many people enjoy dunking into their coffee or milk. This kind of humor is called a pun.

Chapter IV, Part 1:

1. Burning leaves reminds Homer and the sheriff of other things that commonly occur in the fall. What are these fall events? Can you think of others not mentioned?

   Burning leaves reminds them of football, school, and the county fair. Other ideas might include Halloween, Thanksgiving, hay rides, falling leaves, leaves turning color, canning food, or deer hunting.

2. We've already seen that the author likes to have fun with the names of his characters. Can you name four characters found in Greek literature or Greek mythology from which the author has drawn names for the characters of this book? Discuss these characters briefly.

   - ***Homer**: the author of* The Iliad *and* The Odyssey*; Homer was the greatest ancient Greek epic poet, who lived around the 8th century B.C.*
   - ***Ulysses**: the Roman name for Odysseus, the main character in Homer's epic poem,* The Odyssey
   - ***Telemachus**: again, in* The Odyssey*, Telemachus is the son of Odysseus*
   - ***Zeus**: the king of the gods in Greek mythology*

Chapter IV, Part 2:

1. When Miss Terwilliger says she wants to enter the contest, the judge says, "The American female is beginning to find her rightful place in the business and public life of this nation." He is said to have made a "fancy speech about 'woman's rights.'" To what are these sentences referring?

   Women have not always had the same "rights" as men in areas such as voting, property ownership, finances, or marriage. Women used to be completely under the protection and governance of either their fathers or, once married, their husbands. They were not allowed to own property or have a say in politics, and their lives were sometimes sadly affected in ways over which they had no control.

   In America, in the early 1900s, many women in the U.S. began to "fight" for their "rights." They wanted to be able to run for public office, own their own property, and be able to protect themselves, when necessary, from men who wanted to hurt them. This movement is called "woman's suffrage," and grew gradually into the passing of the 19th Amendment in the United States, which gave women the right to vote.

2. Where in the United States is Niagara Falls? For what is it known? Find it on a map.

   Niagara Falls is a series of three large waterfalls located on the border between New York state and the Canadian province of Ontario. The combined falls form the highest flow rate (most powerful) of any waterfall in the world, and are a popular destination for vacationers.

Chapter V, Part 1:

1. After his first impressions, how does the sheriff describe the stranger? Why is this humorous?

   The sheriff describes the stranger as being "shy as a mouse." This is humorous because we find out later in the story that he has built a special mouse trap. He understands how to catch mice because he acts like one himself.

2. Contrast the information people in the story use to "judge" others. What conclusion can you draw?

   The sheriff judges people by their ears, the barber judges by hair, Uncle Ulysses judges by waistline and appetite, Tony the shoe repair man judges by feet and shoes, and the man at the garage judges people by the car they drive. We can draw the conclusion that people tend to judge others based on their own specialized skills. These are the things of which they are most aware and what they notice about others.

3. Homer says Mr. Murphy read that "if a man can make a better mouse trap than anybody else, the world will beat a path to his house." What does this mean? What is the double meaning here?

"Building a better mouse trap" is an idiom that means if a man builds something better than anyone else can build it, people will come to him seeking his skill. The double meaning in this story is that the machine Mr. Murphy builds is literally a ***mouse trap****. However, despite the fact that his machine is better than any others, the world doesn't "beat a path to his house"; he must go out looking for business.*

Chapter V, Part 2:

1. You have learned to be watching for context clues in a story that foretell coming events. Find a clue on page 113 that hints at coming trouble.

After reading up on the effects of music on animals in the library, Homer thinks it would be wise to make some plans for the children's safety. They decide to meet in the school yard on Saturday and arrange a safety signal. Afterwards, Homer repeats, "It's just to be on the safe side." This hints at coming trouble.

Chapter VI, Part 1:

1. Who was Henry Ford, and where did he live? For what is he famous? How does Uncle Ulysses explain the benefits of mass production and assembly lines?

Henry Ford was a pioneer in the automobile industry. He was born and raised on a farm in rural Michigan, but showed skill and interest in mechanics at an early age. He later moved to Detroit to work as an engineer, and eventually formed his own automobile business, the Ford Motor Company. He is famous for introducing the moving assembly line in the making of automobiles, which greatly increased the ability to mass produce cars and make them available to more people at lower costs. Ford's company quickly became the largest automobile manufacturer in the world.

Uncle Ulysses explains mass production, using his doughnut machine as an example. Doughnuts and houses used to be made one at a time, which took longer. But he says now houses can be mass produced quickly, with "modern production genius," just like his machine makes doughnuts.

2. At the end of this section of the chapter, Miss Enders says, "Just think. Last week there were only grass and trees and squirrels on this spot!" Do you think the author is suggesting that this is a good change or a bad one? What do you think?

The author is probably implying that the change is a bad one. He wants the reader to remember what has been destroyed or taken away as a result of building all these new houses. Grass, trees, and squirrels are natural, quiet, and restful, whereas suburbs full of houses and people create more restless activity and noise. Answers will vary.

Chapter VI, Part 2:

1. What items are included in each house in the new suburb? Is this good or bad? Why?

Each new house in the suburb is complete with modern plumbing and kitchens, modern electricity, and is fully furnished. Each yard has plants, sod, a bird house, a revolving clothes line, and a garbage (ash) can. The homes even have sheets, towels, pillow cases, and a picture over the fireplace! Remaining answers will vary.

2. What is a "union"? What problem did the Street Sign Putter Uppers Union cause for Centerburg?

A union is an organization that represents workers in their work place. The union creates rules that aim to protect the rights and good working conditions of their members. Union representatives also often act as a go-between with a company and its workers when there is a disagreement that the two parties cannot settle.

The Street Sign Putter Uppers Union caused a problem for Centerburg by making so many rules and conditions that actually complicated the work and hindered it from being done at all. The rules of the union also made the work more expensive, and caused it to take longer to complete.

QUIZZES & FINAL TEST

(reproducible for classroom use)

Quiz I: Chapters 1-3

Name:____ Date: ____________________ Score: ________

96 pts. total

VOCABULARY: Write the letter of the vocabulary word on the line next to its definition. (20 pts.)

________ 1. machines

________ 2. distrustful

________ 3. challenged

________ 4. one-of-a-kind

________ 5. wavering; shaky

________ 6. criminal

________ 7. disaster

________ 8. used to; familar with

________ 9. tempt

________ 10. famously bad

A. suspicious
B. distinctive
C. quavery
D. calamity
E. devices
F. villain
G. accustomed
H. defied
I. notorious
J. coax

CHARACTER IDENTIFICATION: Match each name below with a character description. (20 pts.)

Homer	Mr. Gabby	Aroma	Uncle Ulysses	Homer's parents
Aunt Agnes	wealthy lady	Freddy	the sheriff	the Super-Duper

1. __________________________ wrecked his car when he dodged a skunk

2. __________________________ a traveling salesman, a "sandwich" man

3. __________________________ Homer's pet skunk

4. __________________________ is impressed with how fast Homer is growing

5. __________________________ is convinced the Super-Duper is a very modest fellow

6. __________________________ has a chauffeur named Charles

7. __________________________ solves problems using common sense

8. __________________________ has a weakness for labor-saving devices

9. __________________________ often mixes up his words

10. __________________________ own and run a tourist camp and service station

WHO SAID THAT?: Write the name of the speaker on the line next to each quotation. (20 pts.)

1. ______________________ "He's an awful modest fellow."
2. ______________________ "We will have to get rid of that animal right away ..."
3. ______________________ "A traveling man in outdoor advertising. I'm a sandwich man."
4. ______________________ "I haven't had so much fun in years. I *really* haven't!"
5. ______________________ "SAY! I know where the bracelet is!"
6. ______________________ "Well, I'll be dunked!!"
7. ______________________ "I didn't want to hit him and get this new car all smelled up."
8. ______________________ "My, how that boy does grow!"
9. ______________________ "Well, I'll be switched."
10. ______________________ "That, my dear friend, is *not* a thing. It is a Musteline Mammal."

SHORT ANSWER: Answer the following questions in complete sentences. (33 pts.)

1. Describe Homer Price, the main character of this story. ______________________

____

____

____

____

2. What is Homer's opinion about comics in general and the Super-Duper? ______________________

____

____

____

____

____

3. How does Homer's common sense help him solve the mystery of the missing bracelet?

____

____

____

____

____

____

Quiz 2: Chapters 4-6

Name:________________________ Date: ______________ Score: ________
96 pts. total

VOCABULARY: Write the letter of the vocabulary word on the line next to its definition. (20 pts.)

________ 1.	stopped	A.	hermit
________ 2.	rapidly, with nervous activity	B.	pied
________ 3.	memory loss	C.	unprecedented
________ 4.	absolutely necessary	D.	replicas
________ 5.	multi-colored	E.	imperative
________ 6.	put a magic spell on	F.	amnesia
________ 7.	never before seen	G.	ideal
________ 8.	one who lives alone	H.	quelled
________ 9.	copies, models	I.	pixied
________ 10.	perfect	J.	frantically

CHARACTER IDENTIFICATION: Match each name below with a character description. (20 pts.)

the barber	Miss Terwilliger	Homer	the librarian	Miss Enders
Uncle Telly	Dulcey Dooner	the judge	the mayor	Uncle Ulysses

1. ________________________ a very clever woman

2. ________________________ hires the stranger to catch all the town's mice

3. ________________________ donates some of her property to build a new suburb

4. ________________________ discovers important information by researching at the library

5. ________________________ refuses to put up street signs unless paid $10 per sign

6. ________________________ warns the sheriff that the town's children may be in danger

7. ________________________ very enthusiastic about mass production and assembly lines

8. ________________________ judges people by their hair

9. ________________________ thinks Miss Terwilliger is a great cook and wants to marry her

10. ________________________ wants to cut expenses by holding a string-saver contest

WHO SAID THAT?: Write the name of the speaker on the line next to each quotation. (20 pts.)

1. ______________________ "I wondered where my jelly beans were disappearing to!"
2. ______________________ "It's marvelous, simply marvelous!"
3. ______________________ "Nope, it's ten dollars or nothing."
4. ______________________ "This is where Ezekiel buried it! And this is where the Homestead stood!"
5. ______________________ "But I don't know how any fine woman could put up with his carryings on!"
6. ______________________ "I think I'll start savin' paper bags or bottle caps!"
7. ______________________ "Isn't it *wonderful* that we have *so* much in common?"
8. ______________________ "That's the principle!"
9. ______________________ "That woman certainly can cook!"
10. ______________________ "Sheriff! Sheriff! Quick! *We guessed the wrong book!*"

SHORT ANSWER: Answer the following questions in complete sentences. (33 pts.)

1. What did Miss Terwilliger do that displayed her cleverness?______________________

____

____

____

____

2. What very important difference is there between Mr. Murphy and the Pied Piper at the end of the chapter?

____

____

____

____

____

3. Describe one benefit and one harmful effect that occurred in Centerburg as a result of mass production.

____

____

____

____

____

____

Homer Price: Final Test

Name:______________________________ Date: ________________ Score: ________
96 pts. total

VOCABULARY: Write the letter of the vocabulary word on the line next to its definition. (10 pts.)

________ 1. challenged		A. accustomed
________ 2. perfect		B. notorious
________ 3. memory loss		C. replicas
________ 4. famously bad		D. calamity
________ 5. one who lives alone		E. amnesia
________ 6. disaster		F. defied
________ 7. copies; models		G. hermit
________ 8. used to; familiar with		H. ideal
________ 9. multi-colored		I. villain
________ 10. criminal		J. pied

CHARACTER IDENTIFICATION: Match each name below with a character description. (10 pts.)

Freddy	Miss Terwilliger	Miss Enders	the librarian	Uncle Ulysses
Homer	the sheriff	Aroma	Mr. Gabby	Uncle Telly

1. ________________________ is convinced the Super-Duper is a very modest fellow

2. ________________________ a very clever woman

3. ________________________ a traveling salesman, a “sandwich” man

4. ________________________ solves problems using common sense

5. ________________________ thinks Miss Terwilliger is a great cook

6. ________________________ has a weakness for labor-saving devices

7. ________________________ warns the sheriff that the town’s children are in danger

8. ________________________ Homer’s pet skunk

9. ________________________ donates some of her property to build a new suburb

10. ________________________ often mixes up his words

WHO SAID THAT?: Match each name to a quotation below and write the name on the line. (10 pts.)

Homer	Miss Terwilliger	Freddy	Aunt Agnes	Miss Enders
Mr. Gabby	Uncle Ulysses	the mayor	Dulcey Dooner	the robber

1. ____________________ "My, how that boy does grow!"
2. ____________________ "Nope, it's ten dollars or nothing."
3. ____________________ "Well, I'll be dunked!!"
4. ____________________ "It's marvelous, simply marvelous!"
5. ____________________ "He's an awful modest fellow."
6. ____________________ "Isn't it *wonderful* that we have *so* much in common?"
7. ____________________ "That, my dear friend, is *not* a thing. It is a Musteline Mammal."
8. ____________________ "SAY! I know where the bracelet is!"
9. ____________________ "I wondered where my jelly beans were disappearing to!"
10. ____________________ "A traveling man in outdoor advertising. I'm a sandwich man."

CHARACTER, SETTING, PLOT: Write a short phrase or sentence to answer each question. (10 pts.)

1. What does the term "character" mean? ____________________

____

____

____

2. Who is the main character in *Homer Price*? ____________________
3. Name three minor characters in *Homer Price*. ____________________

____

____

4. Describe the setting of *Homer Price*. ____________________

____

____

____

5. Tell what the term "plot" means in literature. ____________________

____

____

____

ORDERING EVENTS: Number the events of each chapter in the order in which they occurred. (36 pts.)

Chapter 1

_________ Homer and Aroma find the hideout of the robbers, and Aroma adds his scent to the money.

_________ Homer gathers the robbers' clothes and guns, and marches them to the sheriff.

_________ The award money and lotion from Mr. Dreggs' advertising contest are stolen by four robbers.

_________ When the robbers rent a cabin, Homer recognizes them and reports them to the sheriff.

_________ Aroma is sent into the cabin and frightens the robbers into staying awhile.

_________ Homer finds and tames a skunk, named Aroma, to be his pet.

Chapter 2

_________ The Super-Duper wrecks his car trying to avoid a skunk crossing the road.

_________ The boys pull the car out of the ditch and tow it to Homer's father's garage.

_________ The boys meet Super-Duper at the theater, where he refuses to fly for them.

_________ A fast car speeding around the curve passes the boys driving their horse and wagon.

_________ Super-Duper gives the boys a gift of his comic books.

_________ Homer, Freddy, and Louis look at Super-Duper comic books, but Homer is not impressed.

Chapter 3

_________ Homer offers a reward for the bracelet and tells people it will be found in a doughnut.

_________ A friendly salesman comes to the lunch room for coffee and doughnuts.

_________ The doughnut machine breaks and won't stop producing doughnuts.

_________ Homer and Mr. Gabby think of a way to sell all the extra doughnuts.

_________ The wealthy woman comes back looking for her lost bracelet.

_________ A wealthy woman arrives at the lunch room and offers to make her special doughnut batter.

Chapter 4

_________ The sheriff and Uncle Telly agree to a String Saving contest at the county fair.

_________ Miss Terwilliger surprises everyone and enters the contest herself.

_________ We meet Miss Terwilliger and learn that both Uncle Telly and the sheriff want to marry her.

_________ The men decide that Miss Terwilliger should be the secret "prize" for the contest.

_________ Uncle Telly and Miss Terwilliger are married. The sheriff decides to save bottle caps.

_________ Miss Terwilliger wears her blue dress and wins the contest.

Chapter 5

_________ Mr. Murphy misunderstands the sheriff and releases all the mice back into the town.

_________ All the town's children follow Mr. Murphy as he collects the mice in his amazing machine.

_________ The librarian tells the sheriff "Old Rip" is really more like the Pied Piper, and must be stopped.

_________ Homer learns that "Old Rip" has made a special mouse trap and brings him to the mayor.

_________ Mr. Murphy agrees to catch all the town mice and drive them out of town to release them.

_________ An unusual-looking stranger comes to Centerburg, causing the sheriff to be uneasy.

Chapter 6

_________ Dulcey Dooner is hired to put in much-needed street signs in the new suburb.

_________ One hundred identical houses are built surrounding the old Enders Homestead.

_________ Dulcey Dooner finds the buried Cough Syrup & Elixir Compound, and the homestead is rebuilt.

_________ The homestead is replaced with a new suburban house, and nobody can find their own home.

_________ Miss Enders lives in Centerburg and offers her property to build a new suburb.

_________ Uncle Ulysses is especially interested in mass producing houses and gives lots of advice.

SHORT ANSWER: Write a sentence for each question. (20 pts.)

1. Describe Homer Price, the main character of this story. ______

2. How does Homer's common sense help him solve the mystery of the missing bracelet?

3. What did Miss Terwilliger do that displayed her cleverness? ______

4. What very important difference is there between Mr. Murphy and the Pied Piper at the end of the chapter?

5. Describe one benefit and one harmful effect that occurred in Centerburg as a result of mass production.

QUIZZES & FINAL TEST KEY

Quiz I: Chapters 1-3 Key

Name:______________________________ Date: ________________ Score: ________
96 pts. total

VOCABULARY: Write the letter of the vocabulary word on the line next to its definition. (20 pts.)

E	1. machines	A.	suspicious
A	2. distrustful	B.	distinctive
H	3. challenged	C.	quavery
B	4. one-of-a-kind	D.	calamity
C	5. wavering; shaky	E.	devices
F	6. criminal	F.	villain
D	7. disaster	G.	accustomed
G	8. used to; familar with	H.	defied
J	9. tempt	I.	notorious
I	10. famously bad	J.	coax

CHARACTER IDENTIFICATION: Match each name below with a character description. (20 pts.)

Homer	Mr. Gabby	Aroma	Uncle Ulysses	Homer's parents
Aunt Agnes	wealthy lady	Freddy	the sheriff	the Super-Duper

1. the Super-Duper wrecked his car when he dodged a skunk
2. Mr. Gabby a traveling salesman, a "sandwich" man
3. Aroma Homer's pet skunk
4. Aunt Agnes is impressed with how fast Homer is growing
5. Freddy is convinced the Super-Duper is a very modest fellow
6. wealthy lady has a chauffeur named Charles
7. Homer solves problems using common sense
8. Uncle Ulysses has a weakness for labor-saving devices
9. the sheriff often mixes up his words
10. Homer's parents own and run a tourist camp and service station

WHO SAID THAT?: Write the name of the speaker on the line next to each quotation. (20 pts.)

1. Freddy "He's an awful modest fellow."
2. Homer's mother "We will have to get rid of that animal right away …"
3. Mr. Gabby "A traveling man in outdoor advertising. I'm a sandwich man."
4. wealthy lady "I haven't had so much fun in years. I *really* haven't!"
5. Homer "SAY! I know where the bracelet is!"
6. Uncle Ulysses "Well, I'll be dunked!!"
7. Super-Duper "I didn't want to hit him and get this new car all smelled up."
8. Aunt Agnes "My, how that boy does grow!"
9. sheriff "Well, I'll be switched."
10. (educated) robber "That, my dear friend, is *not* a thing. It is a Musteline Mammal."

SHORT ANSWER: Answer the following questions in complete sentences. (33 pts.)

1. Describe Homer Price, the main character of this story.

   Homer Price is a boy who can solve problems using common sense. He works doing odd jobs at his parents' tourist camp, he plays with other boys, and he enjoys building radios as a hobby.

2. What is Homer's opinion about comics in general and the Super-Duper?

   He is not impressed because he thinks the stories are all too similar, and he realizes that the Super-Duper is just an ordinary man.

3. How does Homer's common sense help him solve the mystery of the missing bracelet?

   He calmly thinks back to where the bracelet was while they were mixing the doughnut batter and when it disappeared. This helps him realize it was accidently mixed into the batter.

Quiz 2: Chapters 4-6 Key

Name:______________________ Date: ______________ Score: ________
96 pts. total

VOCABULARY: Write the letter of the vocabulary word on the line next to its definition. (20 pts.)

Answer	#	Definition		Word
H	1.	stopped	A.	hermit
J	2.	rapidly, with nervous activity	B.	pied
F	3.	memory loss	C.	unprecedented
E	4.	absolutely necessary	D.	replicas
B	5.	multi-colored	E.	imperative
I	6.	put a magic spell on	F.	amnesia
C	7.	never before seen	G.	ideal
A	8.	one who lives alone	H.	quelled
D	9.	copies, models	I.	pixied
G	10.	perfect	J.	frantically

CHARACTER IDENTIFICATION: Match each name below with a character description. (20 pts.)

the barber	Miss Terwilliger	Homer	the librarian	Miss Enders
Uncle Telly	Dulcey Dooner	the judge	the mayor	Uncle Ulysses

1. Miss Terwilliger — a very clever woman
2. the mayor — hires the stranger to catch all the town's mice
3. Miss Enders — donates some of her property to build a new suburb
4. Homer — discovers important information by researching at the library
5. Dulcey Dooner — refuses to put up street signs unless paid $10 per sign
6. the librarian — warns the sheriff that the town's children may be in danger
7. Uncle Ulysses — very enthusiastic about mass production and assembly lines
8. the barber — judges people by their hair
9. Uncle Telly — thinks Miss Terwilliger is a great cook and wants to marry her
10. the judge — wants to cut expenses by holding a string-saver contest

WHO SAID THAT?: Write the name of the speaker on the line next to each quotation. (20 pts.)

1. the mayor — "I wondered where my jelly beans were disappearing to!"
2. Miss Enders — "It's marvelous, simply marvelous!"
3. Dulcey Dooner — "Nope, it's ten dollars or nothing."
4. Homer — "This is where Ezekiel buried it! And this is where the Homestead stood!"
5. Aunt Agnes — "But I don't know how any fine woman could put up with his carryings on!"
6. the sheriff — "I think I'll start savin' paper bags or bottle caps!"
7. Miss Terwilliger — "Isn't it *wonderful* that we have *so* much in common?"
8. Uncle Ulysses — "That's the principle!"
9. Uncle Telly — "That woman certainly can cook!"
10. the librarian — "Sheriff! Sheriff! Quick! *We guessed the wrong book!*"

SHORT ANSWER: Answer the following questions in complete sentences. (33 pts.)

1. What did Miss Terwilliger do that displayed her cleverness?

   When she suspected she was the "prize" of the contest, she entered it herself and found a way to win. She wore her stretchy, blue yarn dress over another dress and unraveled it as she needed more yarn.

2. What very important difference is there between Mr. Murphy and the Pied Piper at the end of the chapter?

   Mr. Murphy is only sad about not getting his money; he doesn't disappear with the children as the piper does.

3. Describe one benefit and one harmful effect that occurred in Centerburg as a result of mass production.

   More houses and modern devices were made available for the people. However, these items were made by a machine and may not be of good quality. There is no interesting variety in this new neighborhood; people have trouble finding their own home.

Homer Price: Final Test Key

Name:____________________________________ Date: __________________ Score: ________

96 pts. total

VOCABULARY: Write the letter of the vocabulary word on the line next to its definition. (10 pts.)

F	1. challenged	A.	accustomed
H	2. perfect	B.	notorious
E	3. memory loss	C.	replicas
B	4. famously bad	D.	calamity
G	5. one who lives alone	E.	amnesia
D	6. disaster	F.	defied
C	7. copies; models	G.	hermit
A	8. used to; familiar with	H.	ideal
J	9. multi-colored	I.	villain
I	10. criminal	J.	pied

CHARACTER IDENTIFICATION: Match each name below with a character description. (10 pts.)

Freddy	Miss Terwilliger	Miss Enders	the librarian	Uncle Ulysses
Homer	the sheriff	Aroma	Mr. Gabby	Uncle Telly

1. Freddy is convinced the Super-Duper is a very modest fellow
2. Miss Terwilliger a very clever woman
3. Mr. Gabby a traveling salesman, a "sandwich" man
4. Homer solves problems using common sense
5. Uncle Telly thinks Miss Terwilliger is a great cook
6. Uncle Ulysses has a weakness for labor-saving devices
7. the librarian warns the sheriff that the town's children are in danger
8. Aroma Homer's pet skunk
9. Miss Enders donates some of her property to build a new suburb
10. the sheriff often mixes up his words

WHO SAID THAT?: Match each name to a quotation below and write the name on the line. (10 pts.)

Homer	Miss Terwilliger	Freddy	Aunt Agnes	Miss Enders
Mr. Gabby	Uncle Ulysses	the mayor	Dulcey Dooner	the robber

1. Aunt Agnes "My, how that boy does grow!"
2. Dulcey Dooner "Nope, it's ten dollars or nothing."
3. Uncle Ulysses "Well, I'll be dunked!!"
4. Miss Enders "It's marvelous, simply marvelous!"
5. Freddy "He's an awful modest fellow."
6. Miss Terwilliger "Isn't it *wonderful* that we have *so* much in common?"
7. the robber "That, my dear friend, is *not* a thing. It is a Musteline Mammal."
8. Homer "SAY! I know where the bracelet is!"
9. the mayor "I wondered where my jelly beans were disappearing to!"
10. Mr. Gabby "A traveling man in outdoor advertising. I'm a sandwich man."

CHARACTER, SETTING, PLOT: Write a short phrase or sentence to answer each question. (10 pts.)

1. What does the term "character" mean? Character means who is in the story.
2. Who is the main character in *Homer Price*? The main character is a boy, Homer Price.
3. Name three minor characters in *Homer Price*. Answers may include: the robbers, Uncle Ulysses, Aunt Agnes, Aroma, sheriff, Freddy, the Super-Duper, Mr. Gabby, Miss Terwilliger, Uncle Telly, Mr. Murphy, Miss Enders, Dulcey Dooner
4. Describe the setting of *Homer Price*. The story takes place in the small town of Centerburg. Some of it takes place at Homer's house, where route 56 meets route 56A.
5. Tell what the term "plot" means in literature. Plot means action or what happens in the story.

ORDERING EVENTS: Number the events of each chapter in the order in which they occurred. (36 pts.)

Chapter 1

__3__ Homer and Aroma find the hideout of the robbers, and Aroma adds his scent to the money.

__6__ Homer gathers the robbers' clothes and guns, and marches them to the sheriff.

__2__ The award money and lotion from Mr. Dreggs' advertising contest are stolen by four robbers.

__4__ When the robbers rent a cabin, Homer recognizes them and reports them to the sheriff.

__5__ Aroma is sent into the cabin and frightens the robbers into staying awhile.

__1__ Homer finds and tames a skunk, named Aroma, to be his pet.

Chapter 2

__4__ The Super-Duper wrecks his car trying to avoid a skunk crossing the road.

__5__ The boys pull the car out of the ditch and tow it to Homer's father's garage.

__2__ The boys meet Super-Duper at the theater, where he refuses to fly for them.

__3__ A fast car speeding around the curve passes the boys driving their horse and wagon.

__6__ Super-Duper gives the boys a gift of his comic books.

__1__ Homer, Freddy, and Louis look at Super-Duper comic books, but Homer is not impressed.

Chapter 3

__6__ Homer offers a reward for the bracelet and tells people it will be found in a doughnut.

__1__ A friendly salesman comes to the lunch room for coffee and doughnuts.

__3__ The doughnut machine breaks and won't stop producing doughnuts.

__4__ Homer and Mr. Gabby think of a way to sell all the extra doughnuts.

__5__ The wealthy woman comes back looking for her lost bracelet.

__2__ A wealthy woman arrives at the lunch room and offers to make her special doughnut batter.

Chapter 4

2 The sheriff and Uncle Telly agree to a String Saving contest at the county fair.

4 Miss Terwilliger surprises everyone and enters the contest herself.

1 We meet Miss Terwilliger and learn that both Uncle Telly and the sheriff want to marry her.

3 The men decide that Miss Terwilliger should be the secret "prize" for the contest.

6 Uncle Telly and Miss Terwilliger are married. The sheriff decides to save bottle caps.

5 Miss Terwilliger wears her blue dress and wins the contest.

Chapter 5

6 Mr. Murphy misunderstands the sheriff and releases all the mice back into the town.

4 All the town's children follow Mr. Murphy as he collects the mice in his amazing machine.

5 The librarian tells the sheriff "Old Rip" is really more like the Pied Piper, and must be stopped

2 Homer learns that "Old Rip" has made a special mouse trap and brings him to the mayor.

3 Mr. Murphy agrees to catch all the town mice and drive them out of town to release them.

1 An unusual-looking stranger comes to Centerburg, causing the sheriff to be uneasy.

Chapter 6

4 Dulcey Dooner is hired to put in much-needed street signs in the new suburb.

3 One hundred identical houses are built surrounding the old Enders Homestead.

6 Dulcey Dooner finds the buried Cough Syrup & Elixir Compound, and the homestead is rebuilt.

5 The homestead is replaced with a new suburban house, and nobody can find their own home.

1 Miss Enders lives in Centerburg and offers her property to build a new suburb.

2 Uncle Ulysses is especially interested in mass producing houses and gives lots of advice.

SHORT ANSWER: Write a sentence for each question. (20 pts.)

1. Describe Homer Price, the main character of this story.

Homer Price is a boy who can solve problems using common sense. He works doing odd jobs at his parents' tourist camp, he plays with other boys, and he enjoys building radios as a hobby.

2. How does Homer's common sense help him solve the mystery of the missing bracelet?

He calmly thinks back to where the bracelet was while they were mixing the doughnut batter and when it disappeared. This helps him realize it was accidently mixed into the batter.

3. What did Miss Terwilliger do that displayed her cleverness?

When she suspected she was the "prize" of the contest, she entered it herself and found a way to win. She wore her stretchy, blue yarn dress over another dress and unraveled it as she needed more yarn.

4. What very important difference is there between Mr. Murphy and the Pied Piper at the end of the chapter?

Mr. Murphy is only sad about not getting his money; he doesn't disappear with the children as the piper does.

5. Describe one benefit and one harmful effect that occurred in Centerburg as a result of mass production.

More houses and modern devices were made available for the people. However, these items were made by a machine and may not be of good quality. There is no interesting variety in this new neighborhood; people have trouble finding their own home.